Behind the Iron Curtain

The story of John Visser as told to A. H. Barbee

Bob Jones University Press, Greenville, South Carolina 29614

Behind the Iron Curtain
by A. H. Barbee

Copyright 1979 by A. H. Barbee
Original edition published by Messenger Ministries
© 1985 Cover Art and Design
Bob Jones University Press
Greenville, SC 29614
ISBN: O-89084-280-9
All rights reserved. No part of this book may be
reproduced in any form, except for brief quotation in a
review, without written permission from the publisher.
Printed in the United States of America

Cover: Elizabeth Brooks Whigham

Contents

Introduction	v
Author's Preface	viii
Map of Places Mentioned in This Book	x
1 God Guides in Communist Lands	1
2 At the Chinese Border	9
3 Paying the Price for Jesus	14
4 More Power in the Gospel Than in Politics	16
5 Communists Are Afraid of the Word of God	19
6 The Power of Prayer in a Communist Country	22
7 A Communist Prison Guard Finds Christ	24
8 People Behind the Iron Curtain	27
9 A Man Without Legs Finds the Solution for His Life	33
10 No Worldly Possessions, But Christ	36
11 Young People Prepared to Follow Jesus	38
12 No Room for Jesus	42
13 Four Plates and Three Guests	45
14 A New Suit and Money for the Lord	47
15 God Be with You Till We Meet Again	49
16 Mrs. Visser Tells Stories	51
Conclusion	63

Introduction

During September 1978, I had the privilege of visiting Hungary and Rumania with Dr. John Visser. I learned firsthand that he has a unique and vital ministry.

Believers behind the Iron Curtain were thrilled to see Dr. Visser. When they greeted him as a brother whom they deeply love, it became apparent to me that he has been a blessing to them for years. Many told me how Dr. Visser has made special trips to perform marriage ceremonies for their children or to conduct funeral services for friends and loved ones who have gone to be with the Lord.

Thousands behind the Iron Curtain look to John Visser as their spiritual leader. He preaches to them, teaches them God's Word, advises them about God's work, and faithfully warns them against apostasy and sin. Dr. Visser is respected as a prophet sent from God, a man performing his ministry as a labor of love.

John Visser is especially qualified for this work. First, the work requires a man who knows the Bible well and preaches it as the Word of God. His keen mind is filled with the truths of theology. But his is not a cold, academic knowledge. He preaches with fervency and power. His messages are filled with illustrations and types from the Word. He meets the requirement given in II Timothy 4:2: "Preach the Word."

Second, a man attempting to work behind the Iron Curtain must be bold. John Visser is as bold as a lion. He fears none but God. Imprisonment and the threat of death have not deterred him in following the course charted by God. Dr. Visser does not scare easily. Using good judgment in all his endeavors, he is careful not to create problems for himself or his fellow believers by unnecessarily antagonizing the atheistic state agents.

I do not know of another man preaching the truths of God's Word with such boldness to those enslaved by Communism. Who else has preached to 1400 people a night in a campaign close to the Russian-Chinese border? What other pastor from another country actually conducts Bible schools for prospective pastors in Poland? Who else conducts evangelistic crusades in the heart of Communist countries, seeing hundreds saved and baptized? Dr. John Visser has surely come to the kingdom for such a time as this.

Ann, his devoted wife, stands firmly with John in his dedication to this work. Saying good-bye to him at the door of their Amsterdam home, she never knows whether she will see him return. While he is away, preparing sermons and preaching, Ann is sewing and providing clothing for destitute families behind the Iron Curtain.

Together the Vissers freely give themselves in loving labor so that a multitude bound by the tyranny of Communism can be set free spiritually. As the Vissers have won the hearts of many living in Iron Curtain countries, they have won a place in mine. While staying in their home and later seeing the needs in so many lands, I thanked God that they listened when He called and that their reply was "Here am I, Lord, send me."

Pastor Ed Nelson
Denver, Colorado

Author's Preface

John Visser is a native of the Netherlands. He founded and for twenty years served as pastor of the largest independent Baptist church in Holland. He was already conducting a successful ministry, which included preaching in the United States and Spain, when God sent him to minister in Communist countries.

He was challenged with the needs of the struggling Christians behind the Iron Curtain by a faithful believer from England. He told Visser that a ministry in countries many Christians consider closed to the gospel message required a special man: a man with a message from God, a man who could speak at least three or four languages, a man having nerves of steel to stand under the constant pressure, a man of good health able to handle harsh climates and strange food.

Visser, who speaks five languages fluently, caught the vision. And after eleven months of prayer he was convinced that he should be God's ambassador of spiritual liberty to lands where grandiose claims of religious freedom are made—but where that freedom is nothing more than a boast. According to Dr. Visser the open churches—mostly liberal or Eastern Orthodox—are merely showcase churches to help build a public image of liberty and tolerance. Leningrad is a good example. Tourist guides gladly tell about nineteen open churches: fifteen Russian Orthodox that don't preach the gospel, one Lutheran church, one Baptist church, one Jewish synagogue, and one other church. But since before Communist control the city had 438 open churches, quite a few have been closed.

In East Germany Visser was once arrested for preaching without permission. His car was confiscated and he was arrested in the Ukraine for bringing Bibles into the country—but only after he had given away 1100. And in Rumania he was arrested and fined for attracting a larger crowd to hear him preach than attended the scheduled village Communist Party meeting.

Reading this account, you will see that the price of being a Christian in Communist lands is high and that the cost of sharing the good news of help and hope to saints and sinners is great.

But John Visser, frequently accompanied by his faithful wife, Ann, forges ahead into Russia, Rumania, Yugoslavia, East Germany, Hungary and Poland, telling the truth BEHIND THE IRON CURTAIN.

A.H. Barbee
San Antonio, Texas

The map shows the major cities and countries mentioned in this account of Dr. Visser's travels.

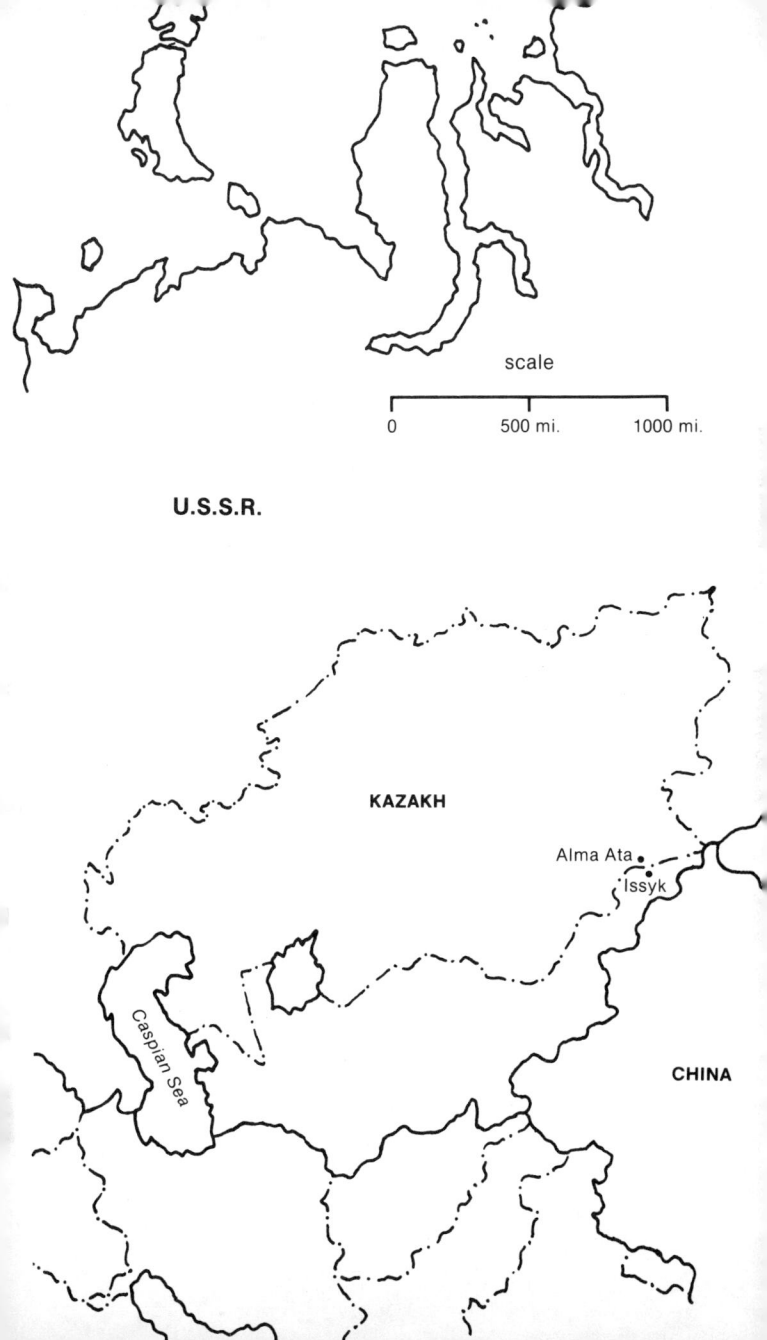

1

God Guides in Communist Lands

Some years ago, shortly after holding revival meetings in Hungary, I received a letter inviting me to preach in Leningrad. It said in part: "I was born in Budapest, Hungary, but when I was three years of age I came to Russia with my parents. Today I am pastor of one of the largest churches here—with about 2000 members. It would be wonderful if you could come to us, too, and have the type of meetings my friend in Budapest told me about."

I prayed about that invitation and decided I should go. When the time came, I flew first to Helsinki, Finland, and then one morning took a boat to Tallinn, Estonia. My usual procedure is to go directly to the border and get a visa at the border. There are several reasons why that is better. However, in Tallinn no visas were available, so that night I had to return on the same boat to Helsinki.

It was Saturday. I settled in a hotel and then phoned the pastor of the Swedish Baptist Church in that city.

He said to me, "It is wonderful that you are here, because tomorrow the Christian students of the university have their farewell. That means all day meetings. If you are here, you'll preach instead of me."

That Sunday was indeed an excellent day for preaching the gospel. But my goal was Russia, not Finland. I told the people in Helsinki that I was sure God wanted me in Russia, but I didn't have a visa. Would they pray that God would open the door?

Most of Sunday night I was up praying to God. The Holy Spirit said to me, "John, you contact the Russian Consul."

I did that the next morning. I phoned and told the Consul of my disappointment. I explained to him that hotel arrangements for my stay in Russia had been made in Holland and all the bills were paid in advance.

"Always before I was granted a visa at the border of socialist countries," I assured him.

He said he was sorry.

"Since you are responsible for Russian affairs in Finland, would it be possible for you to help me?" I asked.

He took some time thinking, and I was praying at my end of the line—he couldn't see that, of course, and at last he said, "Yes, I can help." He gave me the location of the Intourist office and his own secret telephone number. He said, "Just mention that number and it will open a door for you immediately."

I never walked faster in my life than I did

getting over to the Intourist office. There was a crowd of people who wanted to go for one or two days to Estonia. I passed the crowd and said to the lady, "I have come from the Russian Consul. Here is the number."

She turned white, then red, and she said, "What can I do for you, sir?"

I said, "Well, apparently there is some trouble. I was at the border and couldn't get a visa. I have already paid and must go to Russia immediately." This was Monday morning.

She said, "All right, I'll phone."

She phoned and someone told her to help me immediately. So Wednesday morning when I came to her she had the visa all ready in her hands. She said, "Herr Director," that was what was in my passport, "it is all ready now."

I said she did a good job, and I went on the boat again.

On the boat I found the place to eat. There was plenty, but you had to help yourself. One fellow looked at us and took care that we paid. Even in a Communist country nothing is free. We have to pay. When that fellow saw me, he said, "You are here again on the boat?"

"Yes."

"Do you have a visa now?"

"Yes."

"That's impossible in two days. Nobody can get a visa in two days."

"Well," I said to him, "you don't know who I am, sir."

He must have thought I was one of the

leading Communist authorities when I showed him the visa. I was the only one traveling alone on the boat; all the others were in groups.

When we arrived in Tallinn, a lady was there from Intourist. She asked, "Are you Dr. Visser?"

"Yes, lady."

"Your chauffeur and car are ready for you."

"That sounds very good."

They brought me to the Hotel Tallinn where I had paid to stay before I left Holland.

When I arrived at that hotel, I prayed the Lord would open a door for me because my other door had closed. The pastor who invited me had been put out of his church. He had had too many blessings, so he was sent to a very small village where he couldn't do much harm.

There I was in a big town not knowing a soul. But I walked through the town praying that God would direct my steps to the right church. Again at seven o'clock on Sunday morning I walked through the streets. I stopped a young fellow and asked him where a church was. He said, "Around the corner, sir." Sure enough, at quarter past seven there were already 600 people in that church. The meeting was to start at eight o'clock. I couldn't believe my eyes—600 people at quarter past seven.

When I entered that church, one of the elders said to me, "You are a foreigner, sir?"

"Yes."

"Are you a preacher?"

"Yes, sir. You are much better than the rest. They all think I am in business."

He smiled and said, "I'll introduce you to our pastor when he comes in."

The pastor had been sent to Siberia ten years for preaching the Word of God. He was a most gracious man. He said to me, "Dr. Visser, you know how it is here. You cannot preach officially, but you can give greetings to the church. How you do it is up to you."

So I took John 3:16 and I spoke for an hour, giving greetings. Of course, at the end I said I was sorry for taking so long, but I wasn't there every day to greet them.

When they all left the church at ten minutes to ten, I thought that was the end because the church had been full with 1100 seated and some more standing. But at ten o'clock we got another 1100 people, and I started another series of greetings. They said to me I could give the same greetings as before, but I told them there were plenty of greetings in the Book; so I presented another series.

That brought us up to twenty past twelve. Then they said to me, "You know how this church is here. This church has a license, but we also have churches that have no licenses, and they need you very much. But, we should make two things very clear. First, it is a dangerous business. If the officials find out you have preached there they may send you to Siberia. In the second place, we should say they need a man who has a message from God. That you have without a doubt, so think of it."

I said, "All right, I have thought long enough

about it. You'd better send someone to my hotel, and we will go there."

I went to that place, and we were there for three hours that night. There was a Lutheran pastor there, a fine man of God who had been in Siberia and had been beaten so badly that he was more or less an invalid.

They let me preach, and after that they asked me all kinds of Bible questions. That was all.

One of the elders who had been with me, a man sixty-nine years of age, an engineer, said to me, "The pastor is now here."

"What pastor?" I asked.

He mentioned the name of the man who had invited me to Russia. I asked how in the world that was possible.

"Well," they said, "he had a stomach perforation, and in the village where he lived they couldn't help him, so they had to send him here to the hospital."

"Well then, I'm going to see him," I said.

"That would be very difficult because he is under suspicion."

I said, "I'm not bothered about that, sir. I'll be there."

Another man told me the Methodist men should have an official meeting. For that official meeting they needed permission. But the authorities never give permission, not even to sing. Oral Roberts had been there with his choir of young people and had asked to sing one hymn, but they said no. It was not allowed.

I said to the man, "You'd better go to the

Communist who is responsible for all the religion in town and tell him there is a Dutch preacher who wants to preach."

"Well," he said, "I'll try it. You're such a crazy man, I'll go."

I said, "He'll tell you, all right. I have permission."

The man looked at me and left.

The next morning early he came to my hotel smiling. We left the hotel because for several reasons I don't trust them.

He said to me, "The official asked if it was a Dutch preacher. I told him it was, and he said you could preach, but there is one condition."

"What is the condition?" I asked.

"He said that the next morning at ten o'clock I have to go and tell him exactly what you tell us."

"That's a wonderful condition," I said, "because what is good for you is good for the Communists too. You'd better tell him."

After that I went to the hospital where my pastor friend was. A nurse asked who I was, and I told her I came from Amsterdam to visit a friend of mine. They asked me the name, and, when I mentioned it, she said I couldn't see him.

"Well," I said, "you wouldn't tell me that a man who comes all the way from Amsterdam to visit a sick friend here in the hospital couldn't visit him? That's too crazy."

She gave in and said, "All right."

Then something very strange happened. When I came into the hospital room my pastor friend began to weep. He said, "John, How did you get in?"

I told him.

Then the chief of the doctors came to the bed and said, "Well, the pastor is much better now. He can sit up for a moment at a table if you want."

I said, "Sure."

"Are you a pastor too, sir?" the doctor said.

"Yes."

"Since this pastor has been here, we have looked at religion differently. I have many questions. Could I ask you the questions?"

So there we sat around a table in Soviet Russia in a state hospital. Three doctors asked questions on the Bible, and I gave answers and prayed with them. God only could have guided that way. Nobody else could have done this.

When I got home later to the Netherlands, I received a letter from that pastor friend and he said, "My soul is still laughing, when I think of what the Lord has done."

So here is a clear example of the guidance of God in the Communist world today. The God who guided us wants to guide everybody who has given his or her life into the hands of the almighty God.

2

At the Chinese Border

In 1975 I was invited to the Soviet Union by 172 Baptist churches. I went as far as the Chinese border, and in several places they had never seen a preacher from the West since 1917. I believe that is true because when I arrived at twelve o'clock midnight at Alma Ata there were many brothers and sisters. The ladies had flowers, which they presented to me to show their gratitude for coming.

Now, I had the privilege of preaching every day in churches. Some of these were so big that the attendance was 1000 or 1200 in one meeting.

One day I was in a little village where we had about 1000 people. But I was informed that that church was an unregistered church. That means it is a church that does not work one way or another together with the government. They have two primary reasons for rejecting government registration. First, they don't want to send their children to the Communist youth movements like the Pioneers and the Komsomols. Second, they want to baptize the people when they are really saved. In that country no one may be baptized without the permission of the state. The permission is very hard to get, and for those under thirty years of age it is practically impossible. But these people took their children to church with them. The Sunday I was there, twelve people from the church were in prison or in concentration camps, not for political reasons, but because they believed, "Where we are on Sunday, our children should be."

A man who had just spent three years in a concentration camp introduced me with the words, "Blessed is the man who does not walk in the ways of the ungodly."

Now I was very much moved, and I preached as well as I could for about an hour. The people were very, very grateful indeed. I remembered the words of the apostle Paul—"You have accepted me as an angel of God."

I was driven from place to place by car, and I preached along the border of China—on and on and on. Finally the KGB found out what bad things I was doing there—preaching the gospel. One morning a lady knocked at my hotel room. She asked if I would come down.

Two gentlemen from the KGB were waiting for me. Their first question was, "How do you like it here?"

"I like it very much," I said. Naturally I did. I could preach every day, and I am always happy to do that.

Then they said to me, "You have broken the law."

"Which law?" I asked.

"The Soviet law," they said.

"Why is that?" I asked.

"Well," they said, "you have been in Issyk, and you preached there in the church where people have been disobedient to the government. You have permission only to be in Alma Ata."

"Now, sir," I said, "in the first place, when you are in Holland you are not bound to one city. When you come to Amsterdam, you can also go to Rotterdam."

"Well," he said, "this isn't Holland."

One of the men told me again I had broken a law, and for that reason they could arrest me. He threatened me and then said, "In the church where you preached there were many German-speaking Russians who want to go back to Germany. They came here a long time ago, during the days of Catherine the Great. Now they all want to go back. Didn't they say this to you?"

"Yes," I said, "they did."

"What did you say to them?"

"Well, I advised them to stay here."

The policemen liked that because they always want the people to stay. "For what reason?" they asked.

"Well, in the first place, these people are saved, and you are not. They know the way of salvation, and they can show you the way of salvation. Secondly, they are dreamers. They dream about Germany in the days of Martin Luther. But that Germany doesn't exist anymore. For that reason they would be very disappointed. Finally, Germany is a highly industrialized country, and these people are all farmers. These people would all be without work when they get there, so they had better stay here."

They liked the fact that I had advised the people to stay. Then an ominous question was asked.

"What was the color of the car of the man who brought you back to the hotel?"

I told him that it was dark when I was brought back. I had seen the color of the car, but it was true that it was dark, and he accepted the answer. They went on and on questioning. Though I had been arrested three times before, I had the feeling that I had never been nearer to prison than at that moment. But the Lord graciously undertook and at last after more than an hour I stood up and said, "Well, gentlemen, I've nothing to add. I thank you for the talk we've had together." I shook hands with them and left, saying that if they needed me they could always find me in the room.

They didn't come again, but later in Toskand the manager of the hotel where I stayed must have been informed. After he had welcomed me, the first thing he said was that he must give some instructions. I was not allowed to go outside Toskand unless a guide from Intourist went with me. I told him I was very happy for that information because otherwise I would run into great difficulties. After all, I didn't need a guide there. There were twenty-eight churches in and around the city, and I am old enough and wise enough to go on my own. It is not good to have the Intourist people with you because they definitely report on everything you do and say. I never use any political phrases, but still they sometimes misunderstand and turn the words to political purposes.

One of my friends, for instance, had written that you shouldn't trust man, you should trust God. The KGB called him in and accused him for those words. He said he didn't write that, the Psalmist did. They released him that time, but to them his statement was political even if he used the words of the Psalmist.

So it was at the Chinese border that at one church twelve were in prison, yet they were not afraid. They were quite willing to go into a concentration camp for the Lord Jesus Christ. When I asked their leader how it was there with persecution, he said, "It is like the weather. One day sunshine and the next day rain; you can never trust it."

The Christians realized they were in God's hands, even at the Chinese border. Men were willing to go into prison for the sake of Jesus Christ. Would we be willing to do the same?

3

Paying the Price for Jesus

I was in a big town at the Chinese border to preach the Word of God. We had 1400 people at that meeting. What impressed me most was that in a meeting of three hours we had two prayer meetings, each twenty minutes, and that all 1400 people got on their knees. It is unbelievable when you see it. Many prayed. There was a stream of prayer. I believe God is going to listen to the prayers of our persecuted believers there in the Asiatic part of Russia.

At the end of the meeting I saw a lady sitting in a wheelchair—a very old wheelchair. Having been a pastor for so many years, I am interested in people, so I approached the lady and said, "Sister, have you always been an invalid?"

"No," she said, "I have not been. But we had in our church a very capable pastor, and the church grew. The Communists did not like that. One day they tried to get rid of him. They made false accusations, saying that he was immoral, a thief, and other things. To get the idea that the accusation came out of our church instead of from the Communist Party, they came to three of us and urged us to sign a document making these accusations. I refused. Because I refused, they sent me to the concentration camp for seven years. I had to carry heavy loads of wood on my shoulders. I could not do it and broke my back. For that reason I will be in a wheelchair for the rest of my life."

I found out that dear sister had to live on about ten dollars a month. I am happy we can do something for these circumstances. I believe we should help the people who are victims of the system. We should stand by them, for they have paid a price for their stand for Jesus.

I wonder how many in the western world would refuse to sign a false document and refuse to betray their pastor, even if it meant they had to go to a concentration camp for seven years— seven of their best years—doing slavery work. Would they be willing to go with little to eat and poor food, just to remain faithful to the pastor, the man of God. How many would say, "All right, I'll go, and I'll give it into the hands of the Lord, even if I become an invalid"?

When I talked with that lady, I was most impressed. Are we willing to pay such a price for Jesus?

4

More Power in the Gospel Than in Politics

One day my wife and I were doing mission work in a Communist country in eastern Europe. We were in a little village in a church where there was no permission, no license on the building. The church had asked for a license but had not received it.

I preached that night on John 21 and our meeting ran from 8 until 10 p.m. When I was finished, suddenly four policemen came in with their guns. The old pastor and I had to go with them. Ordinarily I hate to travel without my wife, for I think a man without his wife is only half a person. But at that moment I felt sorry for her because of the pressure of this arrest.

Later on, however, she told me that after we left, there was a young man who stood up and said, "Brothers and sisters, all we can do now is pray. Let's pray for Dr. Visser and my father." He was the son of the old pastor. They prayed. After they had a time of prayer, he said, "Let's go quietly home now and trust the Lord." The courage of that young man impressed my wife greatly.

At the police station they took my Bible and, along with other threats, told us that the next day we would have to go to their capital and be put in prison. They told us to be there very early the next morning. When they let us go, I went to the home where we were staying. In those days it was possible to stay in a home. It isn't now. The law says you have to stay in a hotel.

My wife said, "John, shall we leave?"

"No," I said, "because then the believers here would be in even more trouble."

I slept well that night, sleeping on the confidence and promises of the Lord. When I arose the next morning at seven-thirty, the old pastor had already been to the police station and he had my Bible in his hand.

"Oh," he said, "they said I could give it back to you. I have to pay a fine, but we will not be sent to prison."

"That sounds better," I said.

He told me he had to pay $200. That was quite a lot for a pastor who didn't even have $2.00, so I was quite happy to pay for him.

I inquired a little further and asked why the police had come to the meeting. I found out that the Communists had a village meeting for their corporation the same night I was preaching, and only three men had turned up for it. Of course I didn't know about that. So many were in my meeting that the church couldn't hold them, and

17

many stood outdoors. One of the three fellows in the Communist meeting said the others had all gone to church. The Communist leaders went to the police, and the police had to go pick us up.

Later on the Lord turned it for good because the church finally got its license. Now in that place they can gather. We were very grateful to find in that village that there was more power in the gospel than in politics. Almost everyone came to hear the preaching, and only three went to the Communist meeting.

The idea of Communism doesn't really live in the hearts of the people. Many in the Communist world today are willing to listen to the gospel. Believe it, in spite of what you hear; there is more power in the gospel than in politics.

5

Communists Are Afraid of the Word of God

One day we took a carload of Bibles to Russia. After I had given out 1100 Bibles without being hindered, there were still 2000 New Testaments left. I have reason to believe that in the Ukraine I was betrayed.

Suddenly the police were there. They looked and found the New Testaments and then put my co-worker and me in prison for two days and a night. Since everything is so centralized that these people cannot make personal decisions, they immediately telephoned Moscow. What should they do with such criminals? The answer was that they should confiscate my car. Of course I didn't like that, and I said so.

When I protested, I remember one of the men said to me, "You could have come in, but not that Book." He pointed to the New Testament. That made it clear to me that they were afraid of the Word of God. Communists are afraid of the power of the Word of God. They know that when a person accepts the Lord and follows the Book, he will never be a Communist. It is absolutely impossible.

So the car was confiscated and we were sent out of the country (naturally at our own expense). I came home by air. I said to my wife, "The apostle Paul was a Roman citizen. For his rights he went to Rome. I am a Dutch citizen. I will go to The Hague."

So I went to our Ministry of Foreign Affairs and explained the situation. He asked me if I had anything else in the car but the New Testaments, and I told him, "No, sir."

I was told they were going to send a protest through our Dutch ambassador in Moscow. They had never done that before and never afterwards, as far as I know, but they did then on my behalf. In the protest they stated that if a man comes with a car full of books by Karl Marx, we don't steal his car, even if we don't like the Marx books. Naturally, the Communists had to give a reply, so they said I was a smuggler and I don't know what all else.

The story did not stop here, for because of this incident I was interviewed on national television. The reporters asked all kinds of questions. Some of them wanted to talk about political matters, but I always avoid this type of question. One question was, "Do you hate Russians?" I said that was a silly question because I was giving them Bibles free and I preached the gospel to them. Jesus Christ died for Russians and Americans and television reporters.

Then they asked me, "What do you really believe?" I was grateful for nationwide television with two or three million people watching. I told what I believe: that Jesus Christ died for us, that He is risen and is coming again.

The outcome of the program proved that Jesus never fails. That's impossible. Some of the people who heard me speak on television began to send in money for a new car. Two weeks later I had another car, and in another two weeks I was again in eastern Europe. Thus I was enabled to continue the ministry God has given me—preaching and evangelizing the lost and encouraging believers in the Communist world.

On that occasion I did not only go on television, but I also had the privilege of giving long radio messages, which is unusual in my country for a preacher of the gospel. Even the Roman Catholic Broadcasting Company asked me to come speak. And this was even in nearly all leading papers. There were long articles in which I put as much gospel as possible. If I had never believed it before, I believe for sure now what Romans 8:28 says: "All things work together for good to them that love God."

If the Communists are afraid of the Word of God, we who are living as free citizens should value it more and use it and read it and live it for the glory of God.

The Power of Prayer in a Communist Country

God showed us the importance of prayer through a meeting we held in a little village of about 6000. All Christians and other people who were interested in the Word of God came to the meeting, with the result that many had to stand outside. I knew about the police in that country and realized that this was dangerous.

After the meeting, I walked with one of the elders toward my car. About thirty believers followed at a distance. The elder and I said to each other that something could be wrong, so he went back to join the other people and I went on to my car alone. Sure enough, two policemen were there and asked if this was my car. Of course they knew that. Then they asked where I was staying, and I mentioned the hotel. I told them I paid $20 a night for a bedroom. They told me I was in a forbidden district.

I had to go with them to the police station. They telephoned the leaders of their country, asking what to do. Then they began questioning me.

"Why did you come to this district?"

"In my country," I said, "you can travel where you want."

"You can't here," they replied.

They accused me, saying, "Tonight you preached in that church."

I said, "Yes, I did. Is there no religious freedom in your country? You always tell us there is."

"Yes," they said, "there is."

They started phoning again and finally took me back to the car. When they left I went to see the elder, as I knew where he lived. In contrast to most of the people behind the Iron Curtain, he has a rather big house to live in. It is very poor but has big rooms. To my amazement I saw there the thirty people who had followed me. They were all on their knees praying on my behalf.

I saw the power of prayer in that Communist country. Those Christians pray for us also. They prayed for me especially on that occasion, but they pray too for the Christians in the western world. They often ask me if it is true that some Christians are rich. "Isn't it true," they ask, "that there is great danger that they become materialistic? Wouldn't it be good if we would pray for these Christians?" And they do, because the believers in the Communist world believe in the power of prayer.

7

A Communist Prison Guard Finds Christ

Some years ago I had the privilege to lead to the Lord a young man of Albanian background. God spoke to that man in an unusual way, and he started to study the Word of God. The books of the Radio Bible Class of the late Dr. M. R. DeHaan were a great help to him. Being a clever young man, he also started to learn English on his own.

I really came to love that man. He looks on my wife and me as his spiritual parents and even calls us Mother and Father.

After a number of years of good preparation, he went back to his own people and started a work among the Albanians, perhaps the only work among Albanians today. His church is in a very difficult place, near the border of Yugoslavia in a town where you can hardly find a sober man after ten o'clock in the evening. There had never been a mission work or testimony for the Lord before this young man came there. We've been able to encourage this pastor in many ways, particularly in helping finance a new church building there.

Now this man is a faithful and ardent evangelist, even giving out tracts in the street, a dangerous thing to do. One day he was arrested and put in prison for a month. There he started to witness to the prisoners. The authorities didn't like that, so they put him in isolation. But the prisoners began to protest and said he was the only good man there and didn't deserve to be put in isolation. "You should put us there," they said. "He has done no wrong. He has just done good." The authorities had to take him out in order not to have a revolution in the prison.

If you would be with me Sunday morning in his little church of about sixty people, you would find one man who was his prison guard. That prison guard saw and heard the testimony of this prisoner and became so curious that at last he came to church. He accepted the Lord, and now both he and his son are there. That's the way God works sometimes. A Communist prison guard finds Christ because a prisoner was a real witness to the glory of God.

We must ask ourselves if we would be like that Christian if we were under such afflictions because of the gospel. Would we be able to stand that type of persecution—to go into prison for the glory of God?

This pastor said to me, "I wouldn't have missed this for all I have in the world." He has little in this world, and he isn't interested in having much either. He was happy that he was worthy to be in that prison for the glory of God and the furtherance of the gospel.

People Behind the Iron Curtain

One day I was behind the Iron Curtain in a certain country when a man, thirty years of age, came to see me. He said, "I have a great problem. I met a young lady, who is a believer, when she visited our country. We began writing and soon fell in love. Now we want to marry, but she can't come here and I can't go there." She could not live in this country because she is not used to our type of life. He could not join her because he could not get permission to do so legally. So he said, "I have prayed about it, and this is my decision: I will try to escape from this country. But I dare not say so to my father and mother. In the first place, it would break my mother's heart. In the second place, the Communists will come and ask, 'Couldn't you stop him?' If I tell about it, the Communists may punish them in a severe way. If I don't tell them about it, they can truthfully say that they did not know what I was doing. That is why I want to talk it over with you."

So we talked and prayed. The man left the

country. He is in Switzerland now, married and successful. But it is hard. Later I was talking to the parents and they asked me, "Didn't you know?" I had to admit that I did. They said, "We thought you did. Indeed, the Communists did come and ask where our son was. We could say that we didn't know, although we had a good idea that he had left the country."

We had another experience with a young man—the son of a pastor behind the Iron Curtain. He and his fiancee had a great desire to get married, but in that town you can't even get a room to live in and certainly not a house. It happened that in January when snow was on the ground that the fiancee and her mother were kicked out of the only room they had. There they were on the street, mother and daughter. The son of the pastor and his fiancee decided to get out of the country. They got permission from the government tourist department to go to Yugoslavia, but not on a regular visa—on a collective visa. That means as a controlled group.

When they got into Yugoslavia, they escaped to Germany as stowaways on a train, a very dangerous way. The Communists came and took the passports from the whole family so none of them can travel, not even to another Communist country. They can never see their son and will never be able to see the grandchildren. For the rest of their lives they will be separated. It is to Christians in such difficult circumstances that I try to bring comfort.

I have been asked about funerals for believers behind the Iron Curtain. About two or three years ago the father of a pastor in Hungary passed away at ninety-two. He was a great man of God in that church. He and his family desired that I should lead the funeral, so they waited for me. I went in, and we had a tremendous funeral. There must have been five or six hundred people there that day. Many people were at the graveyard—Communists and atheists too, of course. We had some wonderful singing together in the Hungarian language, and then I preached the Word. Later on, some people who were not Christians said, "We have never had such a funeral before. We are used to seeing people weeping, yet here you are all singing."

When a dear brother of ninety-two goes to glory, it is not a cause to weep. He had a long life and he loved the Lord. There are not many prayer warriors like this man, but the Lord will get someone to take his place.

In another case in Rumania a young man died suddenly of a tumor. He was very well known. The funeral was in a small village, but there were one thousand people there. The whole village and many believers from surrounding villages came. We sang hymns and preached the Word of God. It took about three hours all together. But isn't it amazing that kind of testimony can often be used of God to reach atheists? At a funeral you have a special occasion when everybody is attentive. The Communists didn't like it, but we were happy for that opportunity. I would say that life came out of death in that situation.

The Communists now tell us there is a new Soviet man. They had had Communism for such a long time that now something has changed. I must be honest and tell you that I have never met that man. I have met many people, even in the streets of Leningrad, who asked to change my money. People want my money. If you were to compare Communist countries with capitalist countries, I would say it is worse behind the Iron Curtain. You see more hunger. People stand in long lines for a few potatoes. You see ladies working out in the fields, and when you ask them for how much, you find they are there all day long for $1.25. You ask them why they work. They tell you they have to. If they do not work, their garden will be taken away from them. If they have no garden, they can grow no vegetables and will have nothing to give to their children. I sometimes say that is why Jane Fonda didn't stay there but went back to "poor" Hollywood. No man or woman in the western world would like to lead that kind of life. The result is that the women there look much older than they really are. They have such a hard life. They are picked up in a truck at six o'clock every morning, and they work until six o'clock in the evening. After that they have to work at home. So when people tell us that Communism creates better circumstances, I have to tell them that is not true.

Let me give you another example of what

God does sometimes. About ninety-five percent of my journeys are made by car. But one day I went by train to Yugoslavia. In Munich I changed trains and had a sleeper. When I entered the compartment, there was one other man—a leading Communist of Yugoslavia. He was a nice man in his way. I must say that. He introduced himself, told me his profession, and asked what my profession was. I told him I had no profession. The Lord's work should not be called a profession, but a call.

I said to him, "Sir, I have a call."

He asked, "What is that?"

I said, "Well, you are a leading man in your country, and you don't know what a call is?"

He said, "No."

"Did you ever meet a man who was born twice and will never die?"

"No," he said, "I have never met such a man."

"Well," I said, "I am such a man."

"But," he said, "you can't just keep living; you have to die."

I said, "No, sir. That is behind us."

I told him that we died at the cross in Christ. There in that compartment I explained to him the way of salvation and eternal life in the best way I could. I showed him that preaching the gospel of Christ is not a profession but a call.

One day we visited the wife of another leader in a Communist country. The house was excellent. All the people are poor, but not the Communist leaders. My wife, who was with me on that visit, didn't like it because it had to be done in such a secret way. That isn't always good on my wife's nerves. After a long talk the lady accepted the Lord. When her husband heard that she had become a Christian and was even at the church where I was preaching the next Sunday, he became angry, had a heart attack, and died. Today the lady is there alone with her two daughters. But isn't it wonderful that God is willing to save the wife of a Communist leader, if she will listen to the Word of God?

There was a well known-businessman who told me that the Communists came and took all the businesses away. Many of the businessmen committed suicide because the business was all they had lived for. Since he had owned the biggest business in town, I asked about him. How had he felt? "Well," he said, "I realized there are so many things that the Lord has for me in heaven. I have given my business completely into His hands."

He could truly sing what we sing so unthinkingly: "All to Jesus I surrender. All to Him I freely give." He realized he is going to have a new mansion in glory.

Thus there are many ways in which Christians behind the Iron Curtain pay a great price for being faithful to their Lord.

A Man Without Legs Finds the Solution for His Life

My wife and I were in a town behind the Iron Curtain, and I went to a very poor place to preach. While we were walking there with one of our co-workers, a number of people began to follow us, including many Gypsies. They were curious about what would happen. They had never seen such a foreigner there.

So then, people came, we put them all inside and outside the building along with their children, and I started to preach. They had never heard the gospel and in the beginning they laughed. However, soon the Holy Spirit put His seal on the preaching of His Word, and they became silent. I spoke a long time but made it simple so they could understand the message. Finally some of them bowed their heads, and when the time came for the invitation to accept the Lord there were thirteen decisions. I kept the people behind and prayed with every one of them, because I believe I should make it clear what it means when people make a decision.

Now, in that crowd was one man without legs. It was heart-rending to see him brought in on a stretcher. When the invitation was given, a young man wanted to accept the Lord. He lifted up his right hand and then stood on his feet. I always say if someone wants to become a Christian, he should make it clear and open, even there in the Communist world. So this young man had his one hand up and his other hand on the shoulder of the crippled man. He said to that man, "Shouldn't you accept Jesus too, sir?" But he didn't—not that night.

At the end of the meeting some people said, "You should come back here." One Saturday night some time later we were able to return. It was a trip of about a hundred miles in the dark and on a bad road. But we went and, sure enough, in the crowd again there was the man without legs. We had a wonderful meeting, and sixteen people made the decision that night—including the man without legs. He found that Jesus Christ was the answer to his terrible problem of living in this world with his handicap.

There were many children among the Gypsies. My wife, being a good children's worker, gathered all the children in a meeting. She taught choruses and told the way of salvation. And now the children sing, "There is power, power, wonder-working power in the precious blood of the Lamb."

So it is a wonderful place. Twenty-nine people made a decision for the Lord, one man without legs found the solution for his problems, and

Gypsy children heard for the first time the clear preaching of the gospel. We were so grateful to God for leading us to that place.

10

No Worldly Possessions, But Christ

On a certain occasion I went by train to eastern Europe and moved from one place to another either by train or bus. It is hard going, and you can't take anything with you. That is the reason we normally go with our own car. But this time I went by train.

I was told a man would meet me there who could only speak Croatian. That is a language I don't speak. Well, he was there at the station and recognized me because he had heard me preach. He made it clear that I should follow him, so we went to his home.

When we came into his home, I saw what I thought was the kitchen. Only a table and four stools were there—no chairs. I then looked through a window into another room and realized that it was a bedroom. There was only one big bed, and all the other bedclothes were on the floor. He showed me a picture, and I learned he had a wife and eleven children.

The old man could play the guitar. While

waiting for the arrival of a man who could interpret for us, he started to play. He played one song I knew very well. I don't know what your title would be in English, but if I translated it, it would be, "Did You Count the Cost?" "Doesn't your soul have more value than all the riches of the world?" That struck me as I looked around and realized there was no bed for the children. I realized that the value of the man's possessions was not $25. But here was a man with beaming eyes, singing, "Doesn't your soul have more value than all the riches of the world?"

I learned a very good lesson from that man. The riches of the world will pass by, but the value of having Christ in our souls will last for eternity.

Now when I am in that country—and I often go there to preach—that man may come a great distance, giving his last bit of money to be in our meetings. When I look into that man's eyes, I always think of him singing that song. What a rebuke to us who have so much!

11

Young People Prepared to Follow Jesus

Young people in other countries ask what is the price a young person in Communist countries must pay to be a Christian. It is a tremendous price that they pay. Let me give you an example. One day my wife and I were in a Communist country visiting a pastor at whose church I was to preach. He is a leader and a very spiritual man. He has eleven children. The mother is very proud of them and had to show my wife every one of them. Afterward she said to my wife, "We are so happy that your husband is here to preach. But we have to pay a tremendous price these days."

My wife asked, "What is wrong?"

"Today," she said, "my eldest son was sent home from school."

"Why is that?" my wife asked.

"Well," she continued, "he witnessed to a young man that he is a Christian and that the Lord is in his life and so on. That young man went to see the principal of the school."

So this pastor's son was removed from that institute. He will never be able to go to another institute or study at a college or university. He was in what you would call the twelfth grade, and he will never have further opportunity to study. This is part of the tremendous price. Young people, just because they are Christians, cannot have further education.

In that same town behind the Iron Curtain another pastor has a very fine and capable daughter. She was the best in the twelfth grade, and she wanted to study to become a medical doctor. When she went before the committee they didn't ask her much about her knowledge. They knew that. They asked her, instead, how her father lives as a pastor. Where does he get money? Who is supporting him? She said, "That is not a question for me. You should ask my father that question." They said then that she wasn't good enough. She couldn't go to the university.

Once when I was at the University of Moscow, the tourist guide said, "Everybody can study free."

Now that is a marvelous thing to hear, since in countries like America education is expensive. But I said, "Suppose I were a Russian and suppose I were a Christian. Could I study here?"

"No," she said, "If you are a Christian, you can't study here."

So I told her in a loving way that she should not tell people that education is free. She should say that education is free as long as you are not a Christian.

One day I was at the Czechoslovakian border in a church that is rather large for such a small village. At the special youth meeting in connection with my coming, I could hardly believe my eyes. I saw there five hundred young people, mostly between fifteen and twenty-five years of age. Quite a few Americans have seen them in the pictures I have.

My co-worker, a man whom we support through the European Gospel Fellowship, said to me, "How many chairs do you need from the vestry?" He realized I would give an invitation and then would speak personally with those who responded. I told him I would need twenty-three. I must say, though, that deep within my heart I thought that would be too many. To my amazement and to my joy, however, when I gave the invitation, fifty young people stood up and walked down the aisles. I still can hear them pray, "Herr, forgive my sins. Lord, forgive my sin. Lord, make me a child of God."

I was very happy to see this, but I also felt a sorrow. I realized the next day that not one of these young people could go to the university. Before you can study at a university you must sign a set of articles, one of which says that you are an atheist. A Christian can never do that. Another thing I realized was that these young people can never have any promotion in their work.

Nevertheless, fifty out of five hundred were

prepared to follow Jesus at the tremendous cost of no further education and no good job. When I am in the western world, I sometimes wonder if we play church or if we really mean it—especially when we sing, "All to Jesus I surrender, all to Him I freely give." But if in one little village fifty young people are saved and are willing to pay the price in the Communist world, there must be tremendous power in the Word of God.

We can see there is power in what we preach behind the Iron Curtain. What do we preach? We preach the Book, the blood, and the blessed hope. When they heard that message, fifty young people out of five hundred said to Jesus, "Yes, I will follow You all the way."

12

No Room for Jesus

Seven years ago in a Communist country an old lady made a decision for the Lord. She went to a meeting, confessed her sins, and accepted Jesus Christ as the solution to all her problems.

After the meeting she went home. Her husband, who is an ardent Communist, questioned her, "Do you want to say that you became a Christian?"

"Yes," she said, "that's what I want."

"Then," he said, "from this moment there is no room for you. No room for your Jesus." And he sent her out.

Before the Communists took over that country, the farm had belonged to her parents, not to his. Of course now all farms belong to the state, and no one can have a farm of his own. So he sent her out, and she couldn't protest because the Communists would never help her.

What should she do? She went to the pastor and his wife. They are poor people themselves with six children, but they let her come in. I am happy to say that we were able to give them money to build another room attached to that house so she could have a room of her own. She is seventy-six now.

A few months ago my wife said to her, "I'd like to give you a new dress."

"Oh, my dear," she said, "I don't need it. I already have two. I have one for work and one for Sunday. I don't need more. Give it to someone who needs it."

She didn't need more than just these two dresses. However, we did find something she likes very much—to go in the car with us when we travel to preach the gospel. As we drive from village to village to preach, we have taken her with us. One day she said to me, "Now I am in your car, and I could travel with you until the end of the world."

I think of another situation where there was no room for Jesus. I spoke to a Christian woman who lived in just one room. I looked into the eyes of that lady and asked her, "Lady, have you always lived here?"

She said, "No. As far as you can see, the whole street belonged to my husband. The Communists came and took it all from us except one house. When my husband died they came again and said, 'Now you have enough when you have one small room. You can use the kitchen with three others.' "

"But," she said with radiant eyes, "there are many things up in heaven that the Communists can't take from us. So I rejoice in all that He has promised us."

These Christians realize the answer to all their problems is the coming again of the Lord Jesus Christ, for we have a mansion in heaven that will not be touched by any system whatsoever.

There may be no room for Jesus in the world, but there is room for Jesus in the hearts of His people.

13

Four Plates and Three Guests

One day when we were in a Communist country a lady (we call her our Dorcas) said to our co-worker there, "When these missionaries come back, couldn't they come to my home for a meal too? I would love to have them. But" she continued, "I have a great problem, of course. I don't have such good knives and forks and plates."

Knowing they are very poor there, our co-worker smiled and said, "I'll give you good advice and help you. You have a whole year until they come back. In that year you can save enough money for four knives and four forks and four plates." So every month she put a little money aside, and when she had saved enough, she bought a knife or fork or plate.

The great day came. We were there to preach the Word of God, and afterward we went to her home. There was the table on which were laid out the four plates, the four knives, and the four forks. You might suppose that our Dorcas would enjoy the meal with us, but it is the custom in that land for the lady of the house to serve the guests rather than eat with them. I don't like that attitude, but that's how it is. Also, as her husband had to work during the day, only the old grandfather was there. So at the table there were the grandfather, my wife, and I. Though we were only three, she wanted to show what she had, so there were the four places—four plates, four knives, and four forks.

My wife said, "John, for whom would the fourth one be?"

"Well," I said, "it may be for Elijah, you see. It may be ready for him."

We can't understand such circumstances where people have to struggle to save a little money just for knives and forks and plates.

At the end of the meal she insisted on giving a gift to my wife. It was a little gift. My wife, knowing her poverty, felt embarrassed and would not accept it. She began to weep and said, "Why don't you accept it? Don't you like it?"

"I like it, dear," said my wife, "but I don't want to take away what little you have. I feel embarrassed to accept it."

"Oh, no," she said. "You must take it."

Whether my wife wanted to accept it or not, she had to take it. There we had the meal with three persons and four plates and the little present. That is the attitude of the people in the Communist country. I believe we can learn a lot from it.

14

A New Suit and Money for the Lord

Through the years my wife has been busy gathering and buying clothes for poor Christians behind the Iron Curtain. We have two couriers who bring it to them, and, of course, we always take much with us when we travel. On one occasion my wife had noticed a young Christian man who was poor and had no suit. She said she would give a new suit to that young man because he was such a fine Christian. She has the gift of always finding the right measurements. She presented the young man with the suit. He looked nice in it, and he was so grateful.

Later on I heard he had saved a little money all year in order to buy a suit. It wouldn't have been a good quality suit, but it took him all year to save for it, and this even though he was unmarried. But now that he had a new suit from my wife, what should he do with the money?

In his church a man had recently died and left quite a family. Naturally the lady was quite poor. As soon as the young man got the new suit from my wife, he took the little bit of money it had taken the whole year to save and he brought it to the widow. He said, "The Lord has given me a suit now, and I don't need this money for another one, so I want you to have the money to take care of the children."

The only real "communism" I have seen there is among the Christians. That is, people give out of their love and responsibility for their brothers and sisters.

I learned a lesson from these poor people. Here was a new suit and money for the Lord.

15

God Be with You Till We Meet Again

When we go to Communist countries, we usually preach thirty days in one country, thirty days in the next, and so on. One time at the end of thirty days the Christians said to us, "We are going to have a party tonight—a farewell party."

Now, Americans know what a farewell party is. You are very great in suppers. I am afraid that sometimes there are Christians in your country who are more in the Supper Room than in the Upper Room. Anyway, when we had this so-called farewell party, all they gave us at the end was one slice of white bread. Normally they have dark bread. It is very sticky and very bad stuff. Rather than serve this, two ladies who had gone with me to a town where I preached had bought white bread. Along with that slice of white bread we all got a cup of Russian tea, the most horrible drink in the world. Terrible! It seems like grass and water to me. Nevertheless, we drank it.

"Do you often have such parties?" I asked.

"Oh, no," they said, "but every year on New Year's Eve we have it. We come to the church at seven o'clock. We have the party, then we pray, all on our knees. The whole church prays one by one. The men are first and then the ladies." It doesn't matter to them if it takes two and a half hours; they pray to the Lord.

So there we were with a slice of white bread and a cup of Russian tea. The next morning we had to leave around eight o'clock, but these people had to go to work around six. At half past five there they were in one room. A number of Christian men gathered around us to sing "God Be with You Till We Meet Again" before they went to work.

They realize we shall always meet again because Christians never meet for the last time. I hope to meet them several times in their district, if the Lord tarries, preaching to them the riches of our Lord the Saviour. But if I never see them again on earth, I will certainly meet them in eternity because they are trusting Jesus Christ as their Saviour and Lord, even as I do.

16

Mrs. Visser Tells Stories

When we are planning to go behind the Iron Curtain, we have to think about a lot of things. There is much to be bought and much to be done. There is a need for so many items, both small and large. We collect a great deal of second-hand clothing, select what is really good, and take it to the cleaners so it will be clean and neat. What is too worn out, we discard and buy new ones to replace them. There is a great need for pins, thread, needles, string, scissors, clothespins, and many other items. I make a big list and go to the store to buy all those things.

On our previous trip I had promised a lady I would take her a sewing machine. My husband doubted it was wise to do so because we could get in trouble at the Rumanian border. But we were trusting the Lord, and I bought a good electric sewing machine. You cannot buy one good sewing machine in the whole of Rumania. You can buy one in Hungary or Yugoslavia, but they are terribly expensive. You would need to save all your money for a whole year in order to get one. So I promised to buy one in Holland for this lady.

The Lord is always working in a miraculous way. Shortly before we left Amsterdam a friend called on the telephone. He said to me, "Can you take another sewing machine? I have one here."

I looked at my husband, and he said, "I wouldn't do it. It is very dangerous to do it."

"But," I said, "it's awful just to leave it, you know. We are going to take it." So now we had two sewing machines.

When we pack all the things in the car, we like to take as much as possible. So the sewing machines went on the floor behind the front seat and then all the clothes were put in. First the shoes, then the dresses, underwear, and soap. There is a great need for soap, so we make sure we bring a lot of it. We have coffee and tea for the adults and candy for the children in Rumania. The children never get any kind of candy like this. We want to give them something, and they really look forward to getting some chocolate. When we get everything settled in the car, there is hardly room for us.

Someone asked if it is easy for someone to go into such a country. No, it is not. But we trust the Lord. We have many people praying for us in Scotland, Ireland, and America, besides in our own country and the rest of Europe. We are dependent on the Lord.

Before we cross the border, my husband pulls the car aside and prays. He says, "O Lord, we cannot do anything. We are completely dependent on Thee. Help us to take this in." Up till now it is amazing; we haven't had any trouble.

Now, we came with the sewing machines to the check-point at the border. First of all you must change your money. They always love the dollars. They don't like the Americans, but they love the dollars. You have to pay $20 for each day when you enter Rumania. Their money has hardly any value, and you never can change it back. That is no problem for us because we help a lot of people with this money. So we need Rumanian money. It is the same in Hungary. Though it is a little less there, they always make us pay.

Next, the inspector checked the cars. He was checking everything. There were two or three cars in front of us, and he took out every little thing; we saw it with our own eyes. Even when someone had only suitcases, he looked through those. Between the clothes in our car we had many Bibles and hymn books. These were not only from Holland but also from West Germany.

Our turn came. We opened the doors and the trunk ourselves so the inspector could see how many things were in there. But he looked into the car, without taking out one piece, looked at my husband's passport, looked into the car again and said, "All these clothes are not yours alone."

My husband said, "No. Four or five years ago there was a big flood in Rumania, and you asked for help from the western world. We helped a lot of people, so now we have many friends here in your country. Now we have come to visit our friends and help them again. I'm sure you agree with us that when you have so much, you like to share with others. That's what we like to do."

The inspector said, "Yes, yes, that's quite all right." He closed the doors himself without looking through anything else, telling us to have a nice vacation.

We really had a nice vacation, since we had to travel through the countryside. Sometimes the roads are all right. At other times they are so horrible that it takes a long time to get anywhere.

Some years ago you could stay with friends in Rumania, but that is no longer allowed. You stay in hotels. The prices are very high, but you have to do it. Sometimes you come into a place where the hotel is very nice and clean, and the first thing they ask is if you would like to have a bathroom. You say yes, but when you're ready for a bath you find there is no water. You go down and ask the reason, and someone will tell you there is no water. Then you wait a bit, and there is only cold water, not the easiest way to bathe.

It happened that one hotel where we stayed had a door that could not be closed, let alone locked. The bedclothes looked as if twenty people had already slept in them. Everything was smelly and dirty. We asked the man if there was another hotel, and he told us it was ten miles away. He had no personal interest since everything belongs to the state anyway. Whether you sleep in his hotel or not, it doesn't matter to him. He gets about the same pay either way.

We went on to the next hotel as the man suggested. To our amazement it was a real good one. It was clean. There was one bad thing, though. Although it had a bathroom, it could not be used. There is always something out of order, usually because the workers do not care.

We finally arrived at the village where we had promised to take the sewing machine. The first thing we did was hide our car behind a big door. If we had left our car on the street, it would not have worked when we returned to it. Thieves would have taken as much as possible. So we hid our car.

Then we went to see the woman we had come to see. She is the one who helps us distribute the clothes, so we started to take everything out. I said to her, "You see I brought you a sewing machine."

"Oh," she said, "and how is it possible? Did you not have trouble at the border?"

I told her how we came across the border. Then another lady came in, and I said to her, "Mary, I brought you a sewing machine." She started to cry. I told her she shouldn't cry, but laugh.

Then she told me, "This winter I had a sewing machine. It was very old. It broke down, and nobody could repair it. I was so sorry because

I need my sewing machine very much for my family and for others in the church." Believers live close to one another and help each other in every way.

She continued, "I started to pray and said, 'O Lord, help me. Come and bring me another sewing machine.' I thought this was a strange thing to be asking the Lord about and didn't know if He would do it." You can see why we got the second sewing machine and had no trouble in bringing it to her. Though we had no way of knowing about this need, the Lord did.

One time after one of the meetings, a man who brought us to the different places said to us, "Would you like to visit the home of a sick boy? He is sick, and only his mother is a believer. Since she is the only Christian in the home, she may need help and prayer."

As we went to see her, we had to pass the boy, and he was, indeed, very sick. The father was always beside him as much as possible, especially on Sundays. He never went away. He was very sad because his son was so ill.

We went into the kitchen where my husband could speak to the mother. She said, "Do you know, Brother Visser, I asked the Lord, 'Could You not bring me somebody to talk to?' I am so alone, and I don't know anybody who I can speak to right now."

My husband asked if he could speak to the boy. She told us the father never leaves the boy on Sunday. He stays with him the whole day. Then my husband said we would pray that he would leave, because he is a Communist and he would never allow anybody to speak to his boy. So, we started to pray, and the Lord moved the man. When we went into the other room, the man had gone, and my husband had the opportunity to speak to the boy about the Lord. He prayed with him, and the boy was saved.

There was one lady who came to us after the meeting one night and said, "Pastor Visser, when I got ready to come to the meeting tonight, my husband was very angry. He told me if I went to the meeting, I could never go home. He would lock the door, and I would have to sleep in the street."

Then she said, "Will you pray with me?"

It was really a moving sight. All the women were standing around, and my husband began praying for the Lord to help her.

We found out later that when she came home, he just simply let her in. He was quiet and did not say a word. That is the way the Lord works many times.

Sometimes we see the blessings, but we also see the sad things. You may see the children go to school, and then later the door opens and all the children from first grade through third grade come out. I saw this one day and asked, "Where are the children going?"

"Oh," said my friend, "it is harvesttime now. The children have to go to the field and work all day because all the potatoes have to be harvested."

"Do they get any money for this?"

"No," she replied. "They just have to do it. Later on, the newspaper will say the government is so happy because all the children wanted to help in the harvest." It is such a sad thing to see the small ones having to go into the fields to pick up potatoes on their knees all day long.

Another day you may see the high school children. They are clearing the roads, not because they want to but because they have to.

Then there are the funny things we experience. My husband had to sleep in a bed that wasn't strong enough to hold him. It began to bend, and in a moment he fell through it. The people we were staying with were scared. They came into the room to put the bed together, but in a little while he went through it a second time. He told them just to leave it on the floor.

Later at church they came to see him. The woman said to my husband, "Dr. Visser, you can stay with us now because we bought a new bed." You would think nothing of doing that, but they had to save money for a whole year and suffer so much to buy that new bed. But they wanted us and liked to have us in their home so much that they did it anyway.

At one place when we first came, we had to stay in the hotel because the pastor and people were afraid to put us up in their homes. Later, after my husband preached, they came and took the suitcases out of the hotel. They were ashamed that they had not trusted the Lord, and the Lord had spoken to them to have us stay with them.

The person we stayed with was an old shepherd. He was an older man but a very happy one. My husband said to him, "Brother, how is it here on the mountains when you walk with your sheep? Are you very restricted by the Communists?"

"Brother Visser," he said, "even here we are restricted by the Communists. But when I walk with my sheep over the mountains, I talk with the Lord and I walk with the Lord, and it is just heaven to me." You should see his eyes. They shine and sparkle because he is so happy in the Lord.

Later on when his wife prepared a meal for us, we had to sit in the old kitchen on a couple of stools, for there were not any real chairs. The table was covered with things from the sheep because he didn't have anywhere else to put it. Nearly everything in that meal came from the sheep: the meat, the milk, and the cheese. One stool was a hiding place for the bread, so his wife took out of it the bread which she had baked herself. It was dry and hard because she baked only once a week, but she and her husband love to share what they have, and we had a nice meal.

Later on we went to bed. The wife makes everything from wool. She weaves the wool and makes blankets herself and dyes them red. They don't have nice sheets and pillows. She just makes a piece underneath and a piece for the pillow out of the same red wool as the blankets. When we came out of the bed, we were red. It took a while to get it all out. But we were happy that we could stay with them because of their spirit and happiness. We love to be among them.

Another time we stayed in a home with an old pastor. We didn't know how it would go because there was just one little room and a kitchen. In the room there were four beds— three little ones and one very small one.

When we went into the little room, our interpreter had already gone. The lady couldn't speak our language, so she pointed to one bed that I could sleep on. My husband got another bed. She brought in a little boy who got into the small bed, and she and her husband got in the other bed after they had knelt down beside it and praised the Lord. So we all slept in the one room. My husband said just to close our eyes and we would see nothing. That's exactly what we did. To be with these people is always a very, very good thing. Not only do you bring a blessing, but you get a blessing yourself all the time.

We had a meal in another home that had only one room and a kitchen. The lady, who had four children, was a teacher in another area. This was possible because they didn't know in that other area that she was a Christian. After the meal, she asked if we would like to have a little rest since we had two other places to preach. She told us to go lie down on her bed, and she took the children into the kitchen. We had just stretched out a little bit when there came a knock at the door. A brother came in and then another brother and another and another. It wasn't long until there were ten brothers in the room. One of them said, "Brother Visser, we'd like to ask you more questions from the Bible. You can have a rest while we ask you some questions. You are going away in one hour, and we have so many questions."

This is because nothing religious has been printed there in many years. So there we were on the bed resting, and my husband was answering all their Bible questions. It was not much of a rest, but they are so hungry for the Word.

We had the same situation in another place. After the meeting at night a lot of people went to the house where we were to sleep and started asking my husband questions. I went on into the bedroom, but they kept him up until two-thirty in the morning. About seven o'clock I looked out the little window by our bed and said to my husband, "I don't know what is going on, but there are about seven or eight men standing by our door."

We asked our interpreter what was going on, and he said, "The brothers came so early because Brother Visser is going to leave us and they still have more questions from the Bible."

They had come in the night with their hunger for the Word. And they wanted to be there early in the morning to ask more questions because they love the Lord. It really touched our hearts.

We are always traveling, going from city to city and village to village. In this way after so many years the people have come to know my husband. This causes difficulties sometimes because the people in the first village will all walk to the second village the next day to hear him speak. Then, when we move on to the third place, all from the first two villages follow. This means they must go many times through the rain, over bad roads, walking all the way— eight, nine, ten, eleven miles. It doesn't matter to them because they love to listen. However, the meeting room often becomes so crowded that there is hardly enough space for them. Often there is not. Sometimes they take windows out, and people stand outside by the windows. They take blankets and put them around their shoulders so they can stand in the cold and listen to the message. There is such a great hunger over there for the preaching of the Word.

Conclusion

When we read and hear of these things in Communist lands, we must ask ourselves how we compare to these Christians. The day is coming, and it may be soon, when we will have to stand up for the Lord in the face of persecution. Only those people who are fully surrendered to Him have been and will be able to stand as a lighthouse in the darkness today.

Would you be willing to give support to these persecuted believers? The first way to help is to bring to them the Word of God. Another way is to contribute for their material needs. Readers who want to have a part in this ministry to our brothers and sisters behind the Iron Curtain may send their gifts to one of these addresses.

In the United States:

European Christian Fellowship
c/o Engleside Baptist Church
8428 Highland Lane
Alexandria, VA 22309

In Great Britain:

European Christian Fellowship
10 Hayes Gardens
Brumley, Kent,
England
BR2 7DG